TOEFL Vocabulary Quiz Book

Other Kaplan Books for English Learners

TOEFL iBT with CD-ROM, 2008-2009 Edition

Inside the New TOEIC Exam

Inside the TOEFL iBT, Second Edition

TOEFL Idioms Quiz Book

Learn English Through Classic Literature Series

The Short Stories and Essays of Mark Twain

American Tales of Horror and the Supernatural

TOEFL® Vocabulary Quiz Book

KAPLAN) PUBLISHING

New York

© 2008 Kaplan, Inc.

Published by Kaplan Publishing, a division of Kaplan, Inc.
1 Liberty Plaza, 24th Floor
New York, NY 10006

Printed in the United States of America

September 2008
10 9 8 7 6 5 4

ISBN-13: 978-1-4195-5312-7

Kaplan Publishing books are available at special quantity discounts to use for sales promotions, employee premiums, or educational purposes. Please email our Special Sales Department to order or for more information at kaplanpublishing@kaplan.com, or write to Kaplan Publishing, 1 Liberty Plaza, 24th Floor, New York, NY 10006.

HOW TO USE THIS BOOK

The Test of English as a Foreign Language is a standardized test designed to measure your ability to understand and use English as it is used in a North American university setting. Recent changes to the TOEFL have shifted its focus from how much you know about English to how well you comprehend, speak, and write English.

Whether you are taking the TOEFL iBT, TOEFL CBT, or TOEFL Pencil-and-Paper, Kaplan's *TOEFL Vocabulary Quiz Book* is perfectly designed to help you learn over 350 important TOEFL vocabulary words. Simply read the vocabulary word and its part of speech on the front of a page to determine whether you know it; on the reverse side, its definition and a sample sentence are offered to be sure that you understand the word's meaning and its correct, idiomatic usage.

These sample sentences are followed by the corresponding noun, verb, adjective, or adverb forms. Thus you learn an average of four or more new words with each entry and augment your grasp of English grammar as well as your vocabulary. Once you've mastered a particular word, clip or fold back the corner of the flashcard so that you can zip by it to the words you still need to study.

The words are organized according to their part of speech: noun, verb, adjective, or adverb. You will notice, however, that they are not alphabetical. This is to help you focus on the individual word, its meaning, and its context. Words listed alphabetically are harder to distinguish and learn because they look and sound alike.

Study the words in any order and start on any page.

Good luck!

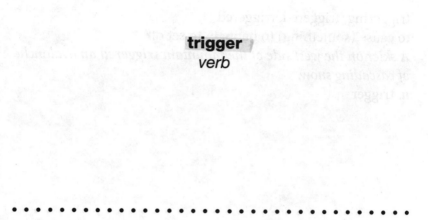

trigger
verb

· ·

volunteer
verb

madelie

triggering, triggered, triggered
to cause (something) to happen, to set off
*A skier on the west side of the mountain **triggered** an avalanche of cascading snow.*
n. trigger

• •

volunteering, volunteered, volunteered
to offer to do something, usually without being asked, pressured, or paid
*When their babysitter canceled at the last minute, I **volunteered** to take care of their son.*
n. volunteer *adj.* voluntary *adv.* voluntarily

predict
verb

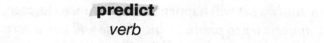

accompany
verb

predicting, predicted, predicted
to know what will happen in the future, to foresee
*Gamblers try to **predict** which horse will win a race.*
n. prediction, predictability *adj.* predictable *adv.* predictably

· ·

accompanying, accompanied, accompanied
to go or come along with
*The Secretary of State **accompanied** the President on his trip.*
n. accompaniment

relax
verb

• •

approve
verb

relaxing, relaxed, relaxed
to become less tense, to slacken
*A massage will help your muscles to **relax**.*
n. relaxation *adj.* relaxing, relaxed

• •

approving, approved, approved
1. to consent to, to allow, or to endorse; 2. to believe to be correct or good
*The treasurer has to **approve** all expenses.*
*His parents don't **approve** of his career choice.*
n. approval *adj.* approving *adv.* approvingly

restrict
verb

• •

violate
verb

restricting, restricted, restricted
to limit, to reduce
*Laws **restrict** the amount of tobacco a person can bring into the country.*
n. restriction *adj.* restrictive *adv.* restrictively

· ·

violating, violated, violated
to defy, to disobey
*By speaking to the press he **violated** our contract.*
n. violation

违反

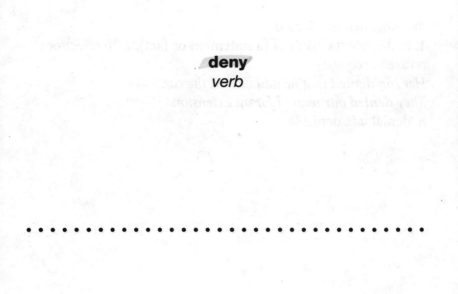

deny
verb

• •

immigrate
verb

denying, denied, denied

1. to dispute the truth of (a statement or fact); 2. to reject or refuse (a request)

*Her son **denied** that he had dented the car.*

*They **denied** our request for an extension.*

n. denial *adj.* deniable

否认

• •

immigrating, immigrated, immigrated

to move to a new country

*Millions of Italians **immigrated** to the United States between 1880 and 1915.*

n. immigration, immigrant

conform
verb

· ·

acknowledge
verb

conforming, conformed, conformed
1. to follow rules or standards; 2. to follow social conventions, to fit in
Your new refrigerator should **conform** *to energy efficiency standards.*
Unlike his free-spirited, artistic sister, he has always tried to **conform**.
n. conformity, conformist *adj.* conformist

• •

acknowledging, acknowledged, acknowledged
to admit or accept as a fact, to recognize
You should **acknowledge** *that your mistakes caused the accident.*
n. acknowledgment *adj.* acknowledged

assemble

verb

• •

expose

verb

assembling, assembled, assembled
1. to put (something) together; 2. to come together
*The engine was **assembled** from spare parts.*
*All students will **assemble** in the cafeteria this afternoon.*
n. assembly

• •

exposing, exposed, exposed
1. to reveal, to uncover; 2. to make vulnerable, to put in contact with something dangerous
*The journalist **exposed** a bribery scandal in the mayor's office.*
*The **explosion** in the factory exposed workers to dangerous chemicals.*
n. exposure, exposé *adj.* exposed

揭露

interpret
verb

• •

demonstrate
verb

interpreting, interpreted, interpreted
to explain or understand the meaning of, to translate
He says that he can **interpret** *people's dreams.*
n. interpretation, interpreter *adj.* interpretive

. . . .

demonstrating, demonstrated, demonstrated
to show, to prove, or to establish (a principle, theory, etc.)
with evidence
Research has **demonstrated** *that this new medication is five
times as effective.*
n. demonstration, demonstrator *adj.* demonstrable, demon-
strative *adv.* demonstrably, demonstratively

adjust
verb

• •

diminish
verb

adjusting, adjusted, adjusted
to change or alter (something) slightly in order to improve it, to modify
*You may need to **adjust** your television antenna for better reception.*
n. adjustment *adj.* adjusted

调整

•••••••••••••••••••••••••••••••••••••

diminishing, diminished, diminished
to become less or worse, to decline
*His influence in the company **diminished** after his successor was chosen.*
adj. diminished, diminishing

acquire
verb

· ·

influence
verb

acquiring, acquired, acquired
to obtain or receive, to attain
During his year in Berlin he **acquired** *a perfect German accent.*
n. acquisition

获得

• •

influencing, influenced, influenced
to have an effect on, to affect, to impact
Current events **influenced** *his recent writing.*
n. influence *adj.* influential, influenced

revise
verb

•••••••••••••••••••••••••••••••••

absorb
verb

revising, revised, revised

1. to reconsider; 2. to improve (a piece of writing, etc.) by changing it

*Upon this discovery, astronomers **revised** their definition of a planet.*

*My teacher told me that if I **revise** the essay I will get a better grade.*

n. revision, revisionism *adj.* revised, revisionary, revisionist

• •

absorbing, absorbed, absorbed

to take in or soak up

*A sponge can **absorb** a lot of liquid.*

n. absorption *adj.* absorbed, absorbing

吸收

purchase
verb

• •

select
verb

purchasing, purchased, purchased
to buy
*They are raising money to **purchase** new computers for the school.*
n. purchase, purchaser

• •

selecting, selected, selected
to choose
*The judges **selected** five dancers as finalists.*
n. selection, selector *adj.* selective, select *adv.* selectively

intervene
verb

. . . .

enhance
verb

intervening, intervened, intervened
to become involved in a situation, to interfere
A fight broke out during the school dance, but the chaperones
***intervened** before anyone was hurt.*
n. intervention *adj.* intervening

· ·

enhancing, enhanced, enhanced
to make better, to improve
*Dressing neatly for a job interview will **enhance** your likelihood*
of getting hired.
n. enhancement *adj.* enhanced

motivate
verb

. . . .

imply
verb

motivating, motivated, motivated
to give (a person) a reason or incentive to do something, to
(encourage) or inspire
Our coach **motivates** *us to practice harder by setting goals.*
n. motive, motivation *adj.* motivated

. . . .

implying, implied, implied
to suggest that something is true without saying so directly, to
(insinuate) 암시하다
Although he didn't complain, his reaction **implied** *that he was*
disappointed.
n. implication *adj.* implicit, implied

reveal
verb

• •

implement
verb

revealing, revealed, revealed
to show, to uncover
*The curtains were pulled back to **reveal** a beautiful view.*
n. revelation *adj.* revealing

揭示 expose

· ·

implementing, implemented, implemented
to put into effect, to enact 通过（法律）
*We will be **implementing** a new grading system next semester.*
n. implement, implementation

贯彻

thrive
verb

• •

strive
verb

thriving, thrived/throve, thrived/thriven
to flourish, to do well, to prosper
*This plant will **thrive** in a warm, wet climate.*

• •

striving, strove/strived, striven/strived
to try, to attempt or endeavor
*She **strove** to be a role model for female athletes.*
n. striver

require
verb

• •

accelerate
verb

requiring, required, required
to need or demand
Finishing a crossword puzzle **requires** *a lot of patience.*
n. requirement *adj.* required

• •

accelerating, accelerated, accelerated
to gain speed, to speed up
The gas pedal makes a car **accelerate.**
n. acceleration

respond
verb

• •

reject
verb

responding, responded, responded
to answer; to reply
Only half of the people we contacted **responded** *to our survey.*
n. response, respondent, responsiveness *adj.* responsive

• •

rejecting, rejected, rejected
to refuse to accept, to dismiss
Very few scientists entirely **reject** *this theory.*
n. reject, rejection *adj.* rejected

derive
verb

• •

invest
verb

deriving, derived, derived
to obtain (something) from a source
*All of the ingredients in this shampoo are **derived** from plants.*
n. derivation, derivative *adj.* derived, derivative

• •

investing, invested, invested
to put money into (stocks, a business, real estate, etc.) in the
hope of making a profit
*He made his fortune by **investing** in the stock market.*
n. investment, investor

investigate
verb

• •

decline
verb

investigating, investigated, investigated
to look closely at (something) in order to <u>determine the truth</u>,
to examine
*The police are **investigating** his connections to organized crime.*
v. investigation, investigator *adj.* investigative

调查

· ·

declining, declined, declined
1. to become lower or worse, to decrease or diminish; 2. to
choose not to do something, to refuse
*The price of gold has **declined** since last year.*
*I **declined** their invitation to dinner.*
n. decline *adj.* declining

下降 衰弱

utilize
verb

· ·

seek
verb

utilizing, utilized, utilized
to use
*Our system **utilizes** the most advanced technology.*
n. utilization, utility

• •

seeking, sought, sought
to look for find
*They are **seeking** applicants for a paralegal job.*
n. seeker

encounter
verb

．．．．．．．．．．．．．．．．．．．．．．．．．．．．．．．．．．．．．．

involve
verb

encountering, encountered, encountered
to meet; to face
*The plans for a new shopping mall **encountered** opposition in the city council.*
n. encounter

. . . .

involving, involved, involved
to make (someone) a part of something
*I don't want to get **involved** with this; it sounds like a terrible idea.*
n. involvement *adj.* involved

anticipate
verb

. . . .

modify
verb

anticipating, anticipated, anticipated
to expect or look forward to *"hope."*
Experts **anticipate** *a major victory by the opposition party in this election.*
n. anticipation *adj.* anticipated, anticipatory

• •

modifying, modified, modified
to adapt; to change or adjust
She **modified** *her car to run on solar power as well as gasoline.*
n. modification *adj.* modified

undergo
verb

• •

underlie
verb

undergoing, underwent, undergone
to experience, to be subjected to
*The website **underwent** a complete remodeling.*

• •

underlying, underlay, underlain   *trigger*
1. to be located beneath; 2. to be a cause or reason for some-thing
*The layer of rock that **underlies** the earth's crust is called the mantle.*
*Numerous issues **underlie** the failure of the peace talks.*
adj. underlying

undertake
verb

• •

translate
verb

undertaking, undertook, undertaken
to attempt, to take on (a task or job); to tackle 处理
*They are **undertaking** a survey of the surrounding land.*

承担

● ●

translating, translated, translated
to interpret, to express in another language
*He is **translating** the plays of Shakespeare into Spanish.*
n. translation, translator

terminate
verb

• •

prohibit
verb

terminating, terminated, terminated
to end, to bring or come to a close
*The landlord **terminated** our rental agreement, so we have to move.*
n. termination

. . . .

prohibiting, prohibited, prohibited
to forbid or ban
*Smoking is **prohibited** in this building.*
n. prohibition *adj.* prohibitive, prohibited

participate
verb

· ·

discriminate
verb

participating, participated, participated
to take part in, to be <u>involved in</u>
*All students are required to **participate** in after-school activities.*
n. participation, participant *adj.* participatory, participating

Intervene

• •

to determine the differen

discriminating, discriminated, discriminated
1. to <u>treat differently</u> because of prejudice; 2. to detect differences, especially small or subtle ones, to differentiate or distinguish
*Universities once **discriminated** against women and minorities in their admissions practices.*
*Newborn babies can't **discriminate** between different colors.*
n. discrimination *adj.* discriminatory, discriminating

comprise
verb

• •

consist
verb

包括

comprising, comprised, comprised
to be made up of, to consist of, to incorporate
*The United States of America **comprises** 50 individual states.*

include

. . . .

consisting, consisted, consisted
to be made up (of)
*A single deck **consists** of 52 playing cards—13 of each suit.*

构成于.

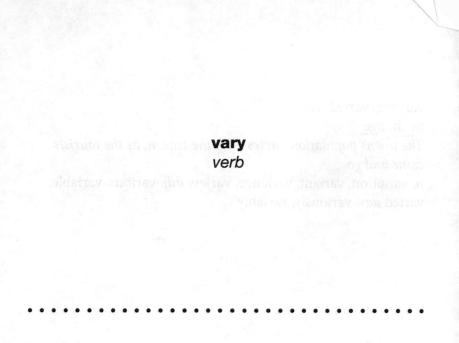

vary
verb

rely
verb

varying, varied, varied
to change
The town's population **varies** *with the season, as the tourists come and go.*
n. variation, variant, variance, variety *adj.* various, variable, varied *adv.* variously, variably

• •

relying, relied, relied
to be dependent (on something)
I **rely** *on the financial aid money to pay for school.*
n. reliance, reliability *adj.* reliant, reliable *adv.* reliably

substitute
verb

. . . .

evaluate
verb

substituting, substituted, substituted
to replace 代替
*The recipe works just as well if you **substitute** oranges for lemons.*
n. substitute, substitution

● ●

评价
evaluating, evaluated, evaluated
to assess, judge, or estimate
*An engineer **evaluated** the condition of the house.*
n. evaluation

outgrow
noun

. . . .

appreciate
verb

outgrowing, outgrew, outgrown
to no longer need or be able to use (something) due to growth
or development
*She used to love this dress but she has **outgrown** it.*

促生长

• •

欣常

appreciating, appreciated, appreciated
to be grateful for
*I really **appreciate** your generous help.*
n. appreciation *adj.* appreciative, appreciable *adv.* apprecia-
tively, appreciably

monitor
verb

· ·

construct
verb

monitoring, monitored, monitored
to observe, to keep track of
*After I got into debt, my parents started **monitoring** my spending.*
n. monitor *adj.* monitored

监视

· ·

constructing, constructed, constructed
to build or form
*The first rule of essay writing is to **construct** a convincing argument.*
n. construction, construct *adj.* constructive, constructed

establish
verb

• •

conclude
verb

establishing, established, established
1. to set up (an institution, etc.), to found; 2. to show that
something is a fact
*Yellowstone Park was **established** in 1872.*
*The prosecutor can **establish** that the defendant was there at
the time of the robbery.*
n. establishment *adj.* established

• •

concluding, concluded, concluded
1. to finish, to end; 2. to develop a judgment after studying or
considering something
*The play **concludes** with a joyful wedding scene.*
*By the end of the meeting, we had **concluded** that your plan
was best.*
n. conclusion *adj.* conclusive, concluded, concluding *adv.*
conclusively

survive
verb

· ·

recommend
verb

surviving, survived, survived
to last or live through an event or period of time, to endure
Only a few books **survived** *the fire in the library.*
n. survival, survivor *adj.* surviving

生存

. . . .

sugesstion not to do somethig.

劝告

recommending, recommended, recommended
1. to advise; 2. to say positive things about, to endorse
The doctor **recommended** *that I avoid salty foods.*
My friend **recommends** *this movie.*
n. recommendation *adj.* recommended

scrutinize
verb

. . . .

pollute
verb

scrutinizing, scrutinized, scrutinized
to closely inspect or examine
*The results were unexpected, but after **scrutinizing** the data we determined it was accurate.*
n. scrutiny

審查

. . . .

又. pollution

broken the environment

polluting, polluted, polluted
to contaminate or make unclean
*The river has been **polluted** by chemicals from the factory.*
n. pollution, pollutant *adj.* polluted

simulate
verb

• •

ensure
verb

simulating, simulated, simulated
to imitate; to mimic 假裝
*Astronauts train in water to **simulate** the experience of weight-lessness.*
n. simulation, simulator *adj.* simulated

· ·

Promise 衛係

ensuring, ensured, ensured
to make (something) certain; to guarantee 保证
*Snow tires should be used in the winter to **ensure** safety on slip-pery roads.*

commence
verb

. . . .

approach
verb

commencing, commenced, commenced
to begin
Construction of the new chemistry building will **commence** *next week.*
n. commencement

• •

approaching, approached, approached
to come close to
Temperatures **approached** *record highs last summer.*
n. approach *adj.* approachable

consult
verb

· ·

distract
verb

consulting, consulted, consulted
to seek advice or information from
You should **consult** *your lawyer before signing a contract.*
n. consultation, consultancy, consultant, consulting *adj.* consultative

●●●●●●●●●●●●●●●●●●●●●●●●●●●●●●●●●

distracting, distracted, distracted
to divert or take away someone's attention
The music is **distracting** *me from my work.*
n. distraction *adj.* distracting

enable
verb

• •

assess
verb

enabling, enabled, enabled
to make able or possible
*A new computer would **enable** us to work faster.*
n. enabler

- -

assessing, assessed, assessed
To judge the nature, quality, or degree of (something), to evaluate or appraise
*Students were asked to **assess** the accuracy of information they found on the Internet.*
n. assessment, assessor *adj.* assessable, assessed

评估

persist
verb

· ·

devote
verb

persisting, persisted, persisted
to last, to go on, to endure
*The bad weather is expected to **persist** for another week.*
n. persistence *adj.* persistent *adv.* persistently

persist in sth / in doing sth
    (with sth).

坚持 / 持续

• •

devoting, devoted, devoted
to commit, to dedicate
*Gandhi **devoted** his life to opposing discrimination and oppression.*
n. devotion, devotee *adj.* devoted *adv.* devotedly

专心

cease
verb

• •

doubt
verb

ceasing, ceased, ceased
to end, to conclude, to stop
*A treaty was signed last night, and the fighting finally **ceased**.*
n. cessation *adj.* ceaseless

• •

doubting, doubted, doubted
to suspect of being untrue
*The police have begun to **doubt** his version of events.*
n. doubt *adj.* doubtful *adv.* doubtfully

precede
verb

unify
verb

preceding, preceded, preceded
to go or come before
*Twenty policemen on motorcycles **preceded** the president's limousine.*
n. precedent, precedence *adj.* preceding

• •

unifying, unified, unified
to bring or come together, to unite
*East and West Germany were **unified** in 1990.*
n. unification, unifier *adj.* unified, unifying

insert
verb

• •

deteriorate
verb

inserting, inserted, inserted
to put (something) into something else
*To start the program, **insert** the disk and follow the instructions.*
n. insertion

插入

• •

deteriorating, deteriorated, deteriorated
to grow worse
*The patient's condition has **deteriorated** since last night.*
n. deterioration *adj.* deteriorating

correspond
verb

. . . .

cooperate
verb

corresponding, corresponded, corresponded
1. to be very similar to something, to match almost exactly; 2.
to exchange letters
*The Greek letter alpha **corresponds** with the letter "A" in the*
Roman alphabet.
*I have **corresponded** with her for several months.*
n. correspondence, correspondent *adj.* corresponding

· ·

With sb / in. on. sth

cooperating, cooperated, cooperated
to work together in order to accomplish something, to col-
laborate
*The United States and Canada **cooperated** to fight smuggling*
over their shared border.
n. cooperation *adj.* cooperative *adv.* cooperatively

协作作

dominate
verb

• •

facilitate
verb

dominating, dominated, dominated
to exert control over
*Our basketball team **dominated** the game.*
n. domination, dominance *adj.* dominant

控制

•••••••••••••••••••••••••••••••

facilitating, facilitated, facilitated
to make (something) easier
*Railroads **facilitated** the settlement of the midwestern United States.*
n. facilitator, facilitation

retain
verb

· ·

complement
verb

retaining, retained, retained
to keep or hold
*The town **retains** much of its historic charm.*
n. retention, retainer *adj.* retentive

• •

补充

complementing, complemented, complemented
to bring out the best in or supply a missing quality to, to be
the ideal partner or accompaniment
*The rich flavor of the wine **complemented** the steak perfectly.*
n. complement *adj.* complementary

compliment
verb

• •

occupy
verb

complimenting, complimented, complimented
to make a positive comment about, to praise
*He **complimented** her excellent taste in music.*
n. compliment *adj.* complimentary

. . . .

occupying, occupied, occupied
1. to be in (a place or position), to inhabit; 2. to engage, em-
ploy, or keep busy
*They **occupied** the house for months without paying rent.*
*The toy **occupied** the boy for hours.*
n. occupancy, occupant, occupier, occupation *adj.* occupied

占用

manipulate
verb

· ·

waive
verb

manipulating, manipulated, manipulated
to influence or control
*He **manipulated** his grandmother into leaving him money in her will.*
n. manipulation, manipulator *adj.* manipulative, manipulated *adv.* manipulatively

. . . .

waiving, waived, waived
to give up, to relinquish
*She **waived** her right to a lawyer.*
n. waiver

convince
verb

• •

perceive
verb

convincing, convinced, convinced
to cause (a person) to agree with a statement or opinion, to persuade
*I finally **convinced** him that I was right.*
adj. convincing, convinced *adv.* convincingly

suppose

. . . .

pay attention

perceiving, perceived, perceived
to sense, to be aware of
*Dogs **perceive** a greater range of sounds than humans can.*
n. perception *adj.* perceived, perceptible *adv.* perceptibly

attribute
verb

•••••••••••••••••••••••••••••••••••

occur
verb

attributing, attributed, attributed
to give credit or assign responsibility for (something) to a
particular person, condition, etc.
*He **attributes** his good health to a low-fat diet and plenty of
exercise.*
n. attribution *adj.* attributable, attributed

把⋯归根于

• •

occurring, occurred, occurred
to happen, to take place
*The burglary **occurred** late last night.*
n. occurrence

intimidate
verb

• •

reinforce
verb

intimidating, intimidated, intimidated
to challenge (a person's) confidence; to make nervous or afraid
His students' knowledge sometimes **intimidates** *him.*
n. intimidation *adj.* intimidating

. . . .

reinforcing, reinforced, reinforced
to make stronger or more intense
He is very close-minded; he only reads books that **reinforce** *his own beliefs.*
n. reinforcement *adj.* reinforced

pursue
verb

. . . .

concentrate
verb

pursuing, pursued, pursued
to follow or chase after
*The dogs **pursued** the fox through the field.*
n. pursuit, pursuer

追求

• •

concentrating, concentrated, concentrated
to <u>focus,</u> to direct one's attention to
*My teacher suggested that I **concentrate** on improving my writing.*
n. concentration

ignore
verb

· ·

detect
verb

ignoring, ignored, ignored
to pay no attention to
*Whenever my little brother annoyed me, my mother just told me to **ignore** him.*
adj. ignored

· ·

detecting, detected, detected
to sense or discover something, to discern, to identify
*I **detected** some uncertainty in her voice as she answered.*
n. detection, detective, detector *adj.* detectable *adv.* detectably

缺陷

expand
verb

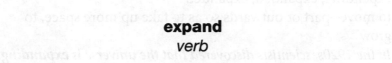

clarify
verb

expanding, expanded, expanded
to move apart or outwards so as to take up more space, to grow
*In the 1920s, scientists discovered that the universe is **expanding**.*
n. expansion, expansionism *adj.* expansive, expanding

• •

clarifying, clarified, clarified
to make something clearer or easier to understand, to explain
*The candidate had to **clarify** his statements about environmental policy.*
n. clarification, clarity *adj.* clarified

compare
verb

• •

react
verb

comparing, compared, compared
to make note of differences and similarities between (two things)
*They **compared** the two cars to see which was the better deal.*
n. comparison *adj.* comparable *adv.* comparably

· ·

reacting, reacted, reacted
to act in response to, to respond
*How did your mother **react** when you told her you were getting married?*
n. reaction *adj.* reactionary, reactive

convey
verb

combine
verb

conveying, conveyed, conveyed
1. to communicate or express; 2. to transport
*She tried to **convey** the seriousness of the situation, but they didn't seem to grasp it.*
*The boxes were **conveyed** to Boston by train.*
n. conveyance

• •

combining, combined, combined
to put together; to blend
*Text messaging **combines** the convenience of e-mail with the speed of a phone call.*
n. combination *adj.* combined

distribute
verb

promote
verb

distributing, distributed, distributed
to give out, to divide among a group
*We **distributed** the money evenly among the group.*
n. distribution, distributor *adj.* distributional

分配

. . . .

promoting, promoted, promoted
1. to support or publicize; 2. to raise (someone) to a higher grade or position
*Actors often go on television talk shows to **promote** their new movies.*
*Jay worked very hard at school, hoping he would be **promoted**.*
n. promotion, promoter

consume
verb

· ·

distort
verb

consuming, consumed, consumed
1. to buy or use up; 2. to eat or drink
*Americans **consume** 25 percent of the world's oil.*
*He **consumed** the entire pie in under ten minutes.*
n. consumer, consumption *adj.* consuming

· ·

distorting, distorted, distorted
to depict something inaccurately
*That mirror **distorts** your image so that you look taller than you are.*
n. distortion *adj.* distorted

Change shape.

eliminate
verb

. . . .

injure
verb

eliminating, eliminated, eliminated
to get rid of, to remove or exclude
*First he became a vegetarian; now he is trying to **eliminate** milk from his diet.*
n. elimination

· ·

injuring, injured, injured
to hurt
*She was badly **injured** in a skiing accident.*
n. injury *adj.* injurious, injured *adv.* injuriously

deplete
verb

· ·

transform
verb

depleting, depleted, depleted
<u>to use up</u>
*Some critics worry that we are rapidly **depleting** the world's oil supply.*
n. depletion

Consume

· ·

transforming, transformed, transformed
to change <u>dramatically</u> 形容
*The discovery of penicillin **transformed** the way doctors treat infections.*
n. transformation

permit
verb

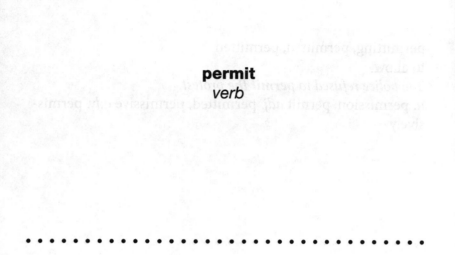

• •

justify
verb

permitting, permitted, permitted
to allow
*The police refused to **permit** the protest.*
n. permission, permit *adj.* permitted, permissive *adv.* permissively

• •

justifying, justified, justified
to show or claim that (something) is right or reasonable
*He tried to **justify** his theft by claiming the money was owed to him.*
n. justification *adj.* justifiable, justified *adv.* justifiably

fluctuate
verb

● ●

deviate
verb

fluctuating, fluctuated, fluctuated 波动
to vary frequently and irregularly, to vacillate
*The temperature has been **fluctuating** a lot recently, so I wasn't
sure if I should wear a coat.*
n. fluctuation *adj.* fluctuating

· ·

违背

deviating, deviated, deviated
to differ or stray from an established standard or course, to
vary or diverge
*The final version of the building **deviated** only slightly from the
original plan.*
n. deviation, deviant *adj.* deviant

export
verb

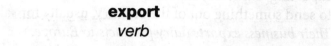

import
verb

exporting, exported, exported
to send something out of the country, usually for sale
*Their business **exports** dairy products to Europe.*
n. exporter, export, exporting *adj.* exported

수입

· ·

수요

importing, imported, imported
to bring something into the country, usually for sale
*He **imports** wine from Europe.*
n. importer, import, importing *adj.* imported

regulate
verb

• •

provide
verb

regulating, regulated, regulated
to control, especially by making rules, to supervise
*The government **regulates** the sale of certain medicines.*
n. regulation, regulator *adj.* regulatory, regulated

implement

. . . .

providing, provided, provided
to supply 提供
*The local bakery **provided** cakes for our bake sale.*
n. provision, provider

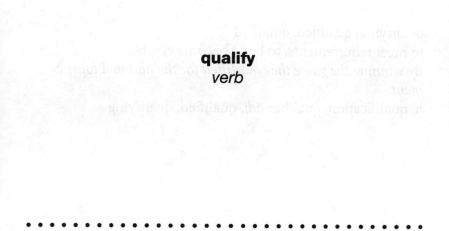

qualify
verb

. . . .

succeed
verb

qualifying, qualified, qualified
to meet requirements, to be or become eligible
*By winning the game they **qualified** for the national tournament.*
n. qualification, qualifier *adj.* qualified, qualifying

● ●

succeeding, succeeded, succeeded
to achieve a goal
*He finally **succeeded** in getting his novel published.*
n. success *adj.* successful *adv.* successfully

remove
verb

. . . .

commit
verb

removing, removed, removed
to take (something) off or away
*You must **remove** the peel before eating a banana.*
n. removal *adj.* removable

• •

committing, committed, committed
1. to promise to do something, to pledge; 2. to carry out (a crime, etc.)
*We **committed** to working here until the end of the summer.*
I never thought I could commit murder.
n. commitment *adj.* committed

generate
verb

· ·

focus
verb

generating, generated, generated
to produce, to create
*Her latest movie has **generated** a lot of controversy.*

. . . .

focusing, focused, focused
to direct one's attention to, to concentrate
*We need to **focus** on the problem of water pollution before it is
too late.*
n. focus *adj.* focused

identify
verb

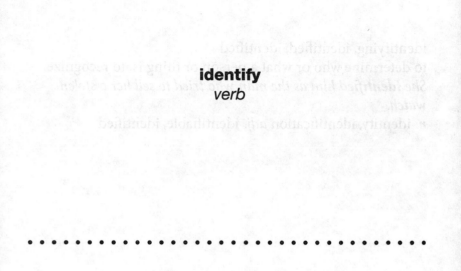

persuade
verb

identifying, identified, identified
to determine who or what a person or thing is, to recognize
*She **identified** him as the man who tried to sell her a stolen watch.*
n. identity, identification *adj.* identifiable, identified

• •

persuading, persuaded, persuaded
to convince
*I was planning to stay here over the vacation, but my parents **persuaded** me to come home instead.*
n. persuasion *adj.* persuasive *adv.* persuasively

organize
verb

• •

tolerate
verb

organizing, organized, organized
1. to put in order; 2. to arrange
*I must **organize** my desk so I can find things more easily.*
*They are **organizing** a concert to benefit local charities.*
n. organization, organizer *adj.* organized

• •

tolerating, tolerated, tolerated
to allow or endure
*My boss doesn't **tolerate** lateness.*
n. tolerance *adj.* tolerant, tolerable *adv.* tolerantly, tolerably

guarantee
verb

· ·

contribute
verb

guaranteeing, guaranteed, guaranteed
to promise or ensure
*Can you **guarantee** that this program will work on my computer?*
n. guarantee *adj.* guaranteed

· ·

contributing, contributed, contributed
to give or donate
*All of the parents were asked to **contribute** twenty dollars for new soccer uniforms.*
n. contribution, contributor *adj.* contributed, contributing

coincide
verb

. . . .

contradict
verb

coinciding, coincided, coincided
to happen at the same time
*Her visit **coincided** with the annual Folk Music Festival.*
n. coincidence *adj.* coincidental *adv.* coincidentally

• •

contradicting, contradicted, contradicted
to oppose or challenge (a person or statement), to dispute
*He **contradicted** your version of the story.*
n. contradiction *adj.* contradictory

recover
verb

• •

perpetuate
verb

recovering, recovered, recovered
to improve after experiencing a decline
*The economy **recovered** quickly after the recent recession.*
n. recovery *adj.* recoverable

· ·

perpetuating, perpetuated, perpetuated
to cause (something) to last indefinitely, to sustain
*Advertisements like these **perpetuate** sexism in our society.*
n. perpetuity *adj.* perpetual *adv.* perpetually

exclude
verb

· ·

estimate
verb

excluding, excluded, excluded
to leave out, to omit
*The boys were **excluded** from the game.*
n. exclusion *adj.* exclusionary, exclusive, excluded *adv.* exclusively

• •

estimating, estimated, estimated
to make an educated guess
*We **estimate** that next year's profits will be 20 percent higher.*
n. estimate, estimation *adj.* estimated

legislate
verb

. . . .

indicate
verb

legislating, legislated, legislated
to make law
*Congress **legislated** a federal minimum wage in 1938.*
n. legislation, legislator, legislature *adj.* legislative *adv.* legislatively

. . . .

indicating, indicated, indicated
to show or suggest
*Your test scores **indicate** exceptional talent in math.*
n. indication, indicator *adj.* indicative

daunt
verb

. . . .

founder
verb

daunting, daunted, daunted
to discourage; to intimidate
*She tried hard not to let the enormity of the situation **daunt** her.*
adj. daunting, daunted

· ·

foundering, foundered, foundered
to sink; to fall helplessly
*After colliding with the jagged rock, the ship **foundered**, forcing the crew to abandon it.*
adj. foundering

goad
verb

. . . .

riddle
verb

goading, goaded, goaded
to prod or urge
*Denise **goaded** her sister Leigh into running the marathon with her.*

• •

riddling, riddled, riddled
to make many holes in; permeate
*The gunfire **riddled** the helicopter with thousands of holes.*

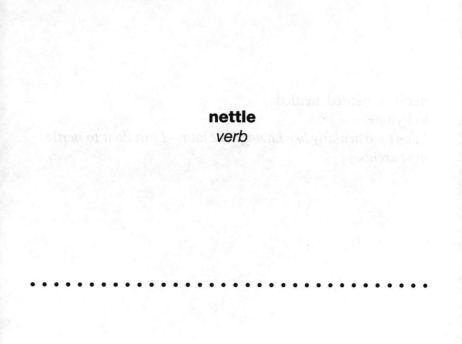

nettle
verb

ply
verb

nettling, nettled, nettled
to irritate
*I don't particularly like having blue hair—I just do it to **nettle** my parents.*

• •

plying, plied, plied
to use diligently; to engage; to join together
*The weaver **plied** the fibers together to make a blanket.*

edit
verb

straightforward
adjective

editing, edited, edited
to change and improve a piece of writing
*Your manuscript is strong, but it needs to be **edited**.*
n. editor, edition *adj.* editorial *adv.* editorially

. . . .

uncomplicated, simple
*An effective speech will be **straightforward** and have a clear point.*
n. straightforwardness *adv.* straightforwardly

preliminary
adjective

• •

valuable
adjective

coming before or done in preparation for something
*Before starting the program, you will need to take a **preliminary** course.*
n. preliminary

. . . .

of great worth, expensive
*The discs contained very **valuable** information.*
v. value *n.* value *adj.* valued

reluctant
adjective

• •

subtle
adjective

unwilling; not eager
*She got the scholarship, but she is **reluctant** to move abroad.*
n. reluctance *adv.* reluctantly

. . . .

delicate or understated, not obvious
*Though garlic can be overpowering, in this recipe it is quite **subtle**.*
n. subtlety *adv.* subtly

vague
adjective

• •

consistent
adjective

unclear, imprecise, not specific
I don't remember exactly what he looked like, but I have a
vague *memory.*
n. vagueness *adv.* vaguely

• •

1. unchanging, stable; 2. compatible, in line with
To train your dog you must be ***consistent*** *about disciplining*
him.
The results of the blood test were ***consistent*** *with the diagnosis.*
n. consistency *adv.* consistently

equivalent
adjective

• •

valid
adjective

equal
*One gallon is **equivalent** to four quarts.*
n. equivalent, equivalence, equivalency *adv.* equivalently

• •

1. acceptable as true; reasonable, convincing; 2. legally binding or effective; legitimate
*She made a very **valid** point about the risks of this investment. He will leave the country soon, because his visa is only **valid** until next week.*
v. validate *n.* validity, validation *adj.* validated *adv.* validly

widespread
adjective

. . . .

rigid
adjective

affecting or existing in a large area; extensive; general
The storm caused **widespread** *damage, with flooding in six states.*

. . . .

hard, stiff, unyielding
There is a **rigid** *dress code at his new school that forbids jeans and sneakers.*
n. rigidity *adv.* rigidly

ultimate
adjective

· ·

abstract
adjective

1. eventual, final; 2. ideal, best
*Her musical career started badly, but her talent and dedication ensured **ultimate** success.*
*This is the **ultimate** chocolate brownie: rich and chewy.*
n. ultimate, ultimatum *adv.* ultimately

• •

based on ideas or general concepts rather than physical reality or specific events
*This aspect of economics seems very **abstract**, but it has important real-life applications.*
n. abstraction, abstract *adv.* abstractly

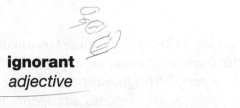

ignorant
adjective

• •

extensive
adjective

lacking in knowledge, unaware, uneducated
*He knows a lot about most sports, but when it comes to hockey he is completely **ignorant**.*
n. ignorance, ignoramus *adv.* ignorantly

· ·

wide-reaching, broad, substantial
*She has **extensive** experience with a variety of computer systems.*
v. extend *n.* extent *adv.* extensively

universal
adjective

• •

positive
adjective

applying to all people or situations
*Fear of the unknown is a **universal** human trait.*
n. universality *adv.* universally

. . . .

good, not negative
*The new rules should have a **positive** effect on safety.*
adv. positively

visible
adjective

. . . .

essential
adjective

able to be seen
*The fish were **visible** through the clear water.*
n. visibility *adv.* visibly

• •

absolutely necessary, crucial
*Good water is **essential** for making good tea.*
n. essence *adv.* essentially

enormous
adjective

· ·

domestic
adjective

immensely large; huge
*The fossil is an **enormous** footprint that may have been made by a dinosaur.*
n. enormity *adv.* enormously

· ·

1. relating to the home or housework; 2. existing, originating or taking place within a particular country
*Women and men today are likely to share the burden of **domestic** tasks.*
*Voters tend to be more interested in **domestic** issues than in foreign affairs.*
n. domesticity, domestic *adv.* domestically

final
adjective

• •

accurate
adjective

last
*Tomorrow is the **final** day of classes for the fall semester.*
v. finalize *n.* finality, finalization, final *adv.* finally

• •

perfectly correct, without errors
*He always checks his bill before paying to make sure it is **accurate**.*
n. accuracy *adv.* accurately

external
adjective

• •

internal
adjective

on or from the outside
*Because no one at the company was able to solve the problem,
an **external** consultant was hired.*
v. externalize *n.* externality, externalization *adj.* externalized
adv. externally

. . . .

on or from the inside
*Technologies such as ultrasound enable doctors to examine
internal organs without surgery.*
v. internalize *n.* internality, internalization *adj.* internalized
adv. internally

rigorous
adjective

• •

profound
adjective

strict, demanding
*Hospitals must maintain **rigorous** standards of cleanliness.*
n. rigor *adv.* rigorously

• •

extremely intense, meaningful or thoughtful
*He has a **profound** understanding of the plight of the poor.*
n. profundity *adv.* profoundly

coherent
adjective

• •

passive
adjective

logical, reasonable and consistent
*To get an A on a paper, you need to have a **coherent** argument and support it with facts.*
n. coherence *adv.* coherently

• •

not actively participating, inactive
*They weren't involved in the vandalism; they were just **passive** witnesses.*
n. passivity *adv.* passively

conceivable
adjective

· ·

adequate
adjective

able to be thought of, imaginable
*We used every **conceivable** method to raise money for the project.*
v. conceive *adv.* conceivably

· ·

of as much quantity or quality as is needed, sufficient, enough
*The climbers left base camp with **adequate** supplies for a three-day journey.*
n. adequacy *adv.* adequately

rapid
adjective

• •

sufficient
adjective

fast, quick
*The ambulance crew has to provide a **rapid** response in emergencies.*
n. rapidity *adv.* rapidly

• •

enough
*The oxygen in the tank is **sufficient** for a one-hour dive.*
v. suffice *n.* sufficiency *adv.* sufficiently

intellectual
adjective

• •

minuscule
adjective

intelligent, relating to intelligence, academic, educated
*She reads a lot, and our conversations are usually very **intellectual**.*
n. intellect, intellectual *adv.* intellectually

. . . .

extremely small; minute; tiny
*The water is safe to drink, but it has a **miniscule** amount of contamination.*

intense
adjective

• •

ambiguous
adjective

extreme, severe
*People with appendicitis experience **intense** abdominal pain.*
v. intensify *n.* intensity, intensification *adj.* intensive, intensified *adv.* intensely, intensively

. . . .

able to be interpreted in more than one way, unclear
*We had a long debate over some **ambiguous** passages in Hamlet.*
n. ambiguity, ambiguousness *adv.* ambiguously

compatible
adjective

• •

medical
adjective

suitable for; able to work with
*His style of acting was more **compatible** with film than with television.*
n. compatibility

· ·

relating to healthcare and the science of treating diseases
*My son wants to get a **medical** degree and become a doctor or nurse.*
v. medicate *n.* medicine *adv.* medically

automatic
adjective

• •

familiar
adjective

that operates or happens on its own, self-activating
*The lights are on an **automatic** timer, so they turn on every
night even if no one is home.*
v. automate *n.* automation *adj.* automated *adv.* automatically

• •

1. acquainted, having knowledge of; 2. well-known, friendly
*I've read many of his books, so I'm **familiar** with his theories.*
*It was good to see a **familiar** face after my long stay abroad.*
n. familiarity

primary
adjective

. . . .

apprehensive
adjective

main, major, most important or significant
*Taxes were one of the **primary** reasons that the American colonies declared independence.*
n. primacy *adj.* prime *adv.* primarily

· ·

nervous, worried that something bad will happen
*He is **apprehensive** about the interview.*
n. apprehensiveness *adv.* apprehensively

mature
adjective

. . . .

annual
adjective

fully grown; aged; adult
*He has become much more **mature** since he went away to college.*
v. mature *n.* maturity, maturation

● ●

occurring once each year; yearly
*I'm taking my car to the mechanic for its **annual** inspection.*
adv. annually

isolated
adjective

· ·

mental
adjective

solitary, alone
*The cabin was completely **isolated** in the middle of the forest.*
v. isolate *n.* isolation, isolationism

• •

relating to the mind, intellectual or psychological
*Her strange behavior led doctors to suspect she was suffering from a **mental** illness.*
n. mentality *adv.* mentally

ethical
adjective

relevant
adjective

concerning or consistent with accepted moral standards, moral

*Doctors disagree about whether it is **ethical** to transplant kidneys from living donors.*

n. ethic *adv.* ethically

. . . .

connected to what is being considered, pertinent, applicable

*The judge ruled that this information wasn't **relevant** to the case.*

n. relevance *adv.* relevantly

prior
adjective

· ·

remarkable
adjective

preexisting, earlier
*Most students in the class have some **prior** knowledge of the subject.*

· ·

noteworthy, striking, extraordinary
*Since the new program began, there has been a **remarkable** increase in the number of applicants to the school.*
adv. remarkably

beneficial
adjective

● ●

infinite
adjective

good, having a positive effect
*Vitamin A is said to be **beneficial** for the eyes.*
n. benefit *adv.* beneficially

. . . .

endless, limitless, innumerable, so great as to be impossible to measure or count
*The universe is so immensely large that many consider it to be **infinite**.*
n. infinity *adv.* infinitely

unique
adjective

· ·

secure
adjective

exceptional, special, one of a kind
*Her style is **unique**.*
n. uniqueness *adv.* uniquely

• •

safe, assured
*Make sure to keep your valuables in a **secure** place.*
v. secure *n.* security *adv.* securely

available
adjective

• •

capable
adjective

readily obtained, possible to get
*This chair is **available** in six different colors.*
n. availability

. . . .

able to do something, competent
*Many scientists still doubt that apes are **capable** of using complex language.*
n. capability

normal
adjective

· ·

integral
adjective

natural, consistent with what is expected
*Is it **normal** for a baby to walk so early?*
v. normalize *n.* normality, normalization *adj.* normalized *adv.* normally

· ·

necessary in order for something to be complete, extremely important
*You are an **integral** part of this project; we couldn't do it without you.*
adv. integrally

comprehensive
adjective

• •

objective
adjective

complete, thorough
*With this **comprehensive** collection of recipes you'll never need another cookbook.*
adv. comprehensively

. . . .

unbiased; unprejudiced
*We need an **objective** judge to tell us whose singing is better.*
n. objectivity *adv.* objectively

temporary
adjective

· ·

significant
adjective

lasting a short time
*This won't work forever; it's only a **temporary** solution.*
adv. temporarily

. . . .

worthy of attention, important, remarkable
*There has been a **significant** increase in the annual number of forest fires.*
n. significance *adv.* significantly

maximum
adjective

• •

minimum
adjective

of the greatest possible amount or degree, most
*I got a ticket for driving over the **maximum** speed.*
v. maximize *n.* maximum, maximization *adj.* maximal *adv.*
maximally

• •

of the least possible amount or degree
*They set a **minimum** GPA of 3.5 for applicants to the honors
program.*
v. minimize *n.* minimum, minimization *adj.* minimal *adv.*
minimally

considerable
adjective

ethnic
adjective

great in amount or extent, sizable, substantial, significant
*The first European colonists in North America faced **considerable** hardships during the cold winter months.*
adv. considerably

• •

cultural, united or defined by culture, tradition, or nationality
*The event was intended to promote understanding between members of different **ethnic** groups.*
n. ethnicity *adv.* ethnically

legal
adjective

• •

previous
adjective

allowed by or relating to the law, lawful

*Alcoholic beverages were banned in the United States from 1919 until 1933, when prohibition ended and they became **legal** again.*

v. legalize *n.* legalization, legality *adj.* legalized *adv.* legally

• •

prior

*Do you have any **previous** experience?*

adv. previously

distinctive
adjective

• •

contrary
adjective

characteristic, special, unique
*Asparagus has a **distinctive** taste.*
n. distinction *adj.* distinct *adv.* distinctively, distinctly

• •

opposite, contradictory, conflicting
*No matter what I say, you always argue the **contrary** position.*
n. contrary *adv.* contrarily

stable
adjective

• •

inevitable
adjective

unlikely to change or shift, secure
*It is best for children to grow up in **stable** homes.*
v. stabilize *n.* stability, stabilization *adv.* stably

. . . .

impossible to prevent, unavoidable
*He was a dangerous driver, and it was **inevitable** that he would eventually get into an accident.*
n. inevitability *adv.* inevitably

obvious
adjective

• •

mutual
adjective

easily seen or recognized; clear
*It was **obvious** that she was going to win.*
adv. obviously

. . . .

shared by or affecting both parties
*My parents made a **mutual** decision to sell the house.*
adv. mutually

brief
adjective

• •

fundamental
adjective

short
*There will be a **brief** announcement before class today.*
n. brevity *adv.* briefly

· ·

basic, essential, intrinsic
The Supreme Court has recognized that all citizens have a
***fundamental** right to privacy.*
n. fundamental *adv.* fundamentally

random
adjective

. . . .

rational
adjective

without order or organization
*The seating assignments were **random**.*
n. random, randomness *adv.* randomly

• •

consistent with logic and reason, reasonable, logical
*A good judge must be **rational**, and not easily swayed by emotion.*
v. rationalize *n.* rationality, rationalization, rationalist *adv.* rationally

. . . .

similar
adjective

incredible
adjective

resembling something else, alike
*Oranges and tangerines are **similar** fruits.*
n. similarity *adv.* similarly

· ·

hard to believe, amazing, remarkable
*He has an **incredible** ability to learn new languages quickly.*
adv. incredibly

predominant
adjective

. . . .

liable
adjective

strongest or most prevalent, foremost, main, primary
*The cake is supposed to be chocolate mocha, but the **predominant** flavor is coffee.*
v. predominate *n.* predominance *adv.* predominantly

• •

legally responsible
*Parents are **liable** for damage caused by their children.*
n. liability

identical
adjective

• •

neutral
adjective

exactly the same
*We hoped the other airline would be cheaper, but the ticket prices were **identical**.*
adv. identically

. . . .

belonging to neither of two opposing categories, impartial, unaffiliated
*I am liberal, but my brother is conservative, so to avoid offending either of us my mother tries to be politically **neutral**.*
v. neutralize *n.* neutrality, neutralization *adj.* neutralized *adv.* neutrally

appropriate
adjective

· ·

global
adjective

proper or suitable
*Some parents worry that these video games may not be **appropriate** for children.*
n. appropriateness *adv.* appropriately

● ●

relating to or affecting the entire world, widespread
*After years of operating locally, we have decided to become a **global** company serving people in many countries.*
n. globe, globalization *adv.* globally

mediocre
adjective

· ·

mandatory
adjective

of moderate quality or ability, unexceptional, passable
*She's an excellent guitarist but only **mediocre** as a drummer.*
n. mediocrity

. . . .

required, obligatory, compulsory
*Before the start of classes, new students must attend a **mandatory** orientation.*

deceptive
adjective

· ·

intrinsic
adjective

misleading, giving a false impression
*The pictures were **deceptive**—the apartment was actually quite small.*
v. deceive *n.* deception *adv.* deceptively

• •

deeply rooted, essential, inherent
*Freedom of expression is an **intrinsic** American value.*
adv. intrinsically

contemporary
adjective

• •

complex
adjective

1. existing or happening at the same time; contemporaneous;
2. existing or happening in the present, modern
*His childhood was **contemporary** with the First World War.*
*Their house is filled with fashionable **contemporary** furniture.*
n. contemporary

. . . .

difficult to understand, complicated
*The problem was too **complex** to be solved in a single meeting.*
n. complexity

crucial
adjective

• •

intermediate
adjective

extremely important, indispensable
The helicopter is delivering **crucial** *supplies to a remote hospital.*
n. crux *adv.* crucially

• •

situated between two stages, in the middle
Before moving on to the advanced class, I am going to try the
intermediate *level.*

glib
adj

stoic
adj

said in an insincere manner; offhand, casual
*The slimy politician managed to continue gaining supporters because he was a **glib** speaker.*

. . . .

indifferent to or unaffected by emotions
*While most of the mourners wept, the dead woman's husband kept up a **stoic**, unemotional facade.*

potential
noun

. . . .

overview
noun

ability or promise
*Her coach thinks she has the **potential** to be a world-class athlete.*
adv. potentially

. . . .

a general survey
*This book offers an **overview** of the major developments in astronomy since the time of Galileo.*

phenomenon
noun

· ·

foundation
noun

plural: *phenomena*
something that exists or occurs, especially something remarkable, an occurrence, a wonder
The annual migration of the monarch butterflies is an incredible natural **phenomenon**.
adj. phenomenal *adv.* phenomenally

• •

the base that something is built on; basis; underpinning
Charles Darwin's theory of natural selection is the **foundation** *of modern biology.*
adj. foundational

evidence
noun

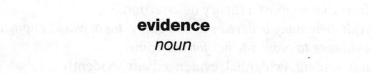

option
noun

facts that support a theory or assertion
Although many believed she was guilty, there wasn't enough **evidence** *to prosecute her for the crime.*
adj. evident, evidential, evidenced *adv.* evidently

• •

a choice or possibility
There are several different **options** *for getting Internet access.*
adj. optional *adv.* optionally

insight
noun

• •

logic
noun

understanding or appreciation
*This book gave me greater **insight** into modern politics.*
adj. insightful *adv.* insightfully

• •

reason; rational thinking
*The problem has to be solved with **logic**.*
n. logician *adj.* logical *adv.* logically

statistic
noun

• •

publication
noun

information derived from numerical analysis
The latest **statistics** *show an increase in the rate of population growth.*
n. statistician *adj.* statistical *adv.* statistically

· ·

1. the act of publishing a text; 2. a published book, journal, magazine, etc.
He is excited about the **publication** *of his first novel.*
She has written articles for several different **publications**.

error
noun

. . . .

method
noun

a mistake
*This report contains an unacceptable number of **errors**.*
v. err *adj.* erroneous *adv.* erroneously

● ●

a way of doing something, a technique
*They are developing a new **method** for learning to read music.*
n. methodology *adj.* methodical, methodological *adv.* methodically; methodologically

revolution
noun

• •

commerce
noun

1. a circular movement, a rotation or turn; 2. a dramatic change, especially the overthrow of a government
Earth completes a **revolution** *around the sun every 365¼ days. The American* **Revolution** *overthrew an English colonial government; the French* **Revolution** *unseated a native ruling class.*
v. revolve, revolutionize *n.* revolutionary, revolt *adj.* revolutionary

• •

economic activity, trade, business
The new policies are supposed to encourage **commerce** *by helping small businesses.*
adj. commercial *adv.* commercially

administration
noun

. . . .

conflict
noun

1. the group of people responsible for managing a company, government, etc.; management; 2. the act of administering
*The proposal has to be approved by the University **administration**.*
*She is going to business school to get a degree in **administration**.*
v. administer, administrate *n.* administrator *adj.* administrative *adv.* administratively

• •

a state or incident of disagreement or hostility, a clash
*There is often a **conflict** between one's personal desires and the best interest of society.*
v. conflict *adj.* conflicting, conflicted

partner
noun

· ·

innovation
noun

one who shares an activity, business, etc.
*She's looking for a new tennis **partner**.*
n. partnership

. . . .

a new way of doing something, an invention
*The VCR was a major **innovation** in the way people watched films.*
v. innovate *n.* innovator *adj.* innovative *adv.* innovatively

finance
noun

· ·

behavior
noun

1. the field of banking and investments; 2. (in plural) a person's or company's situation with respect to money
My brother is a stockbroker, and I also plan to have a career in **finance**.
My **finances** *are very bad right now, and I am afraid the bank will reject my loan application.*
v. finance *n.* financier, financing *adj.* financial *adv.* financially

● ●

the way that a person acts, conduct
They criticized his **behavior** *during the game.*
v. behave *adj.* behavioral *adv.* behaviorally

prerequisite
noun

● ●

phase
noun

something that must be done beforehand, a requirement or precondition
*Introductory English 101 is a **prerequisite** for the advanced creative writing course.*
adj. prerequisite

• •

a stage
*Before becoming a butterfly, a caterpillar goes through a "chrysalis" **phase**.*

wisdom
noun

• •

candidate
noun

knowledge and good judgment based on experience; good sense
The decision demonstrated her **wisdom**.
adj. wise *adv.* wisely

. . . .

a person seeking a position, especially a person running for election to public office
She is one of three **candidates** *for Governor.*

status
noun

• •

ideology
noun

importance in relation to others, rank
*People often judge the social **status** of others based on the way they dress.*

• •

a strong and rigid system of belief; dogma
*The Communist **ideology** was very influential during the twentieth century.*
n. ideologue *adj.* ideological *adv.* ideologically

location
noun

. . . .

controversy
noun

a position or site, a place
*They still haven't found a good **location** for their new restaurant.*
v. locate *adj.* located

. . . .

intense public disagreement about something, a debate
*A **controversy** arose over the school's new science curriculum.*
adj. controversial *adv.* controversially

incentive
noun

• •

outcome
noun

a reward for doing something
*To attract new members, the gym is offering **incentives** such as free yoga classes.*

• •

a result
*The **outcome** of the election was a surprise to everyone.*

proficiency
noun

• •

instance
noun

ability, skill, competence
Before studying abroad, students are expected to achieve basic **proficiency** *in a foreign language.*
adj. proficient *adv.* proficiently

• •

an example of an action or phenomenon; an occurrence; an occasion
It was just one more **instance** *of personal failure.*

gender
noun

• •

concept
noun

the sex (male or female) of a person
*Discrimination based on **gender** is illegal.*
adj. gendered

· ·

an idea, especially one that is abstract and general
*As an introduction, she explained the major **concepts** that
would be covered in the class.*
v. conceptualize *n.* conception, conceptualization *adj.* concep-
tual, conceptualized *adv.* conceptually

diversity
noun

. . . .

leeway
noun

1. variety, especially in terms of culture or ethnicity; 2. multi-formity

*The **diversity** of the student body has increased significantly in the past decade.*

*Scientists fear that climate change will lead to less **diversity** of animal and plant species.*

v. diversify *n.* diversification *adj.* diverse, diversified *adv.* diversely

* *

flexibility, freedom, room for variation or to maneuver

*The camp counselors were given a lot of **leeway** in how they chose to enforce the rules.*

resource
noun

. . . .

proof
noun

a stock of information, skill, money, etc., that can be used to make or accomplish something
*Do you have enough **resources** to carry out this project?*
adj. resourceful

• •

evidence showing that a statement or fact is true, verification
*New customers are required to show **proof** that they live in the neighborhood.*

opportunity
noun

· ·

alternative
noun

a chance to do something
*The recital will give her an **opportunity** to demonstrate her talent.*
adj. opportune *adv.* opportunely

. . . .

any of multiple options, another possibility
*Whole grains such as barley are exciting and healthy **alternatives** to pasta.*
adj. alternative *adv.* alternatively

majority
noun

. . . .

minority
noun

the largest part of a whole, over half
*The **majority** of Americans prefer coffee to tea.*

· ·

1. a small part of a whole, less than half; 2. a member of a group that accounts for less than half of a population
*Atheists are a **minority** in the United States.*
*The company is recruiting **minorities** for positions on its board of directors.*

talent
noun

. . . .

data
noun

natural skill or ability
*He has an amazing **talent** for music.*
adj. talented

. . . .

singular: *datum*
information
*The report is based on **data** collected over 25 years.*

media
noun

narrative
noun

singular: *medium*
the news and entertainment outlets such as the press, television, radio, and film
The politician was unhappy with the way he had been depicted in the media.

• •

a story, an account of connected events
*The Odyssey is a long **narrative** in the form of a poem.*
v. narrate *n.* narration *adj.* narrative *adv.* narratively

tactic
noun

· ·

symbol
noun

a plan or technique for achieving a goal, a strategy
*The new **tactics** introduced by our coach helped us win the game.*
n. tactician *adj.* tactical *adv.* tactically

. . . .

an image, etc., that represents something else; a sign
*The raven in the poem is often interpreted as a **symbol** of death.*
v. symbolize *n.* symbolism *adj.* symbolic *adv.* symbolically

duration
noun

· ·

expert
noun

the length of time that something lasts
*Please remain seated for the **duration** of the flight.*

• •

a person who has special knowledge or experience in a particular field
*The museum called in an **expert** to determine if the painting was a forgery.*
n. expertise *adj.* expert *adv.* expertly

labor
noun

• •

bias
noun

work, especially physical work
*Without a ride-on mower, mowing your lawn can be exhausting **labor**.*
v. labor *adj.* laborious *adv.* laboriously

• •

an attitude that is unfairly positive or negative about a particular group, person, or thing in comparison to others; prejudice
*The company is accused of **bias** against the elderly in its hiring practices.*
adj. biased

decade
noun

• •

genre
noun

a period of ten years
The Great Depression of the 1930s lasted an entire **decade**.

· ·

a style or category, especially a type of literature, etc.
He prefers books in the **genre** *of science fiction.*

perspective
noun

• •

text
noun

a point of view
*I'd like to hear your **perspective** on this issue.*

● ●

a piece of writing
*The class will discuss **texts** by six major twentieth-century thinkers.*
adj. textual

trend
noun

· ·

function
noun

a dominant pattern or direction; a tendency
*The **trend** towards larger and larger vehicles has begun to change.*

• •

what something is used for; purpose or utility
*Archaeologists are uncertain about the **function** of these ancient stone tools.*
v. function *n.* functionality *adj.* functional, functioning *adv.* functionally

comment
noun

• •

lecture
noun

a remark that expresses an observation or opinion
*We never had a chance to give our **comments** on the proposal.*
v. comment *n.* commentary, commentator

● ●

a speech intended to teach something
*Are you going to Professor Smith's **lecture** on the Cold War?*
v. lecture *n.* lecturer

emphasis
noun

analysis
noun

plural: *emphases*
special attention, stress, prominence
The new laws put **emphasis** *on protecting the environment.*
v. emphasize *adj.* emphatic *adv.* emphatically

· ·

plural: *analyses*
a detailed interpretation of information
An **analysis** *of the test results showed gradual improvement in math scores.*
n. analyst *v.* analyze *adj.* analytical, analyzed *adv.* analytically

hypothesis
noun

· ·

circumstance
noun

plural: *hypotheses*
an unproven theory, especially a scientific one
Her **hypothesis** *was that the mice eating the special diet would grow twice as fast.*
v. hypothesize *adj.* hypothetical *adv.* hypothetically

• •

a condition or fact that affects an event or creates a situation
The room was cold and dark, and she hadn't slept the night before; it is difficult to take a test under those **circumstances**.
adj. circumstantial

strategy
noun

tradition
noun

a plan for how to do something; a method
*In chess, it is important to have a strong **strategy** from the beginning of the game.*
v. strategize *n.* strategist *adj.* strategic *adv.* strategically

• •

a practice or belief that has existed for a long time; a custom
*Our family has a **tradition** of eating fish for dinner on Christmas Eve.*
n. traditionalist *adj.* traditional *adv.* traditionally

regime
noun

• •

target
noun

a government, usually one that is oppressive and authoritarian
Her book discusses the various groups that opposed the Nazi
regime*.*

● ●

something that is aimed for; a goal
*To meet our **target**, we have to increase sales by 15 percent.*
v. target *adj.* targeted

era
noun

authority
noun

a long period in history that has defining characteristics
*She recommended a book about the colonial **era**.*

. . . .

the power or right to make decisions or judgments about something
*Only Congress has the **authority** to officially declare war.*
adj. authoritative *adv.* authoritatively

generation
noun

hierarchy
noun

all of the people who are born within a particular period of
time
*The **generation** of Americans born right after World War II are
often called the "baby boomers."*

. . . .

a fixed order of things by status or importance
*There was a strict **hierarchy** in medieval European society, with
the king at the top and the peasants on the bottom.*
adj. hierarchical *adv.* hierarchically

income
noun

· ·

assumption
noun

money that is paid to a person or company; salary; earnings
*If she gets promoted, her **income** will increase substantially.*

● ●

a belief that is not based on proof
*Historians must be careful not to make **assumptions** about the past based on today's values.*
v. assume *adj.* assumed

priority
noun

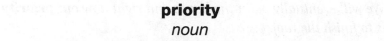

summary
noun

something considered to be of the highest importance
*We will eventually paint the house, but right now our **priority** is to finish the roof.*
v. prioritize *n.* prioritization

· ·

a short description of the content of a longer piece of writing, film, etc.
*We were asked to write a one-page **summary** of the book.*
v. summarize *n.* summarization *adj.* summarized

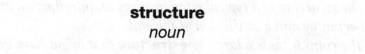

structure
noun

· ·

theory
noun

1. the way in which the parts of something are put together; organization 2. a building or construction
*The **structure** of a typical essay involves an introduction at the beginning and a conclusion at the end.*
*The ruins include a large, low **structure** that might have been used to store grain.*
v. structure *adj.* structural, structured *adv.* structurally

• •

a system of ideas that is meant to explain a complex phenomenon; a belief, thesis, or hypothesis
*Scientists are developing new **theories** about the nature of the universe.*
v. theorize *n.* theorist *adj.* theoretical *adv.* theoretically

revenue

noun

• •

appearance

noun

income; money that is earned
*The store has had much higher **revenues** this year.*

• •

the way something looks
*It is a beautiful old house, but the broken windows ruin its **appearance**.*
v. appear *adj.* apparent *adv.* apparently

climate
noun

· ·

research
noun

weather conditions over a long period of time; the environment

*Scientists are studying the forces causing changes in the **climate**.*

adj. climatic

· ·

intensive study of a particular topic

*She is doing **research** on local history.*

v. research *n.* researcher

impact
noun

. . . .

challenge
noun

an impression, an effect
*The film had a great **impact** on me; I was really moved.*
v. impact *adj.* impacted

. . . .

1. a difficult task or undertaking; 2. a questioning of authority
*The marathon is a **challenge** even for experienced runners.*
*Impressionist paintings were seen as a **challenge** to traditional artistic standards.*
v. challenge *n.* challenger *adj.* challenging, challenged

individual
noun

. . . .

region
noun

a single person

*Identical twins often complain that people tend to treat them as a pair, rather than as **individuals**.*

n. individuality, individualism, individualist *adj.* individual, individualistic, individualized *adv.* individually

· ·

a large area that is considered to have unifying characteristics

*The southwestern **region** of the United States is known for its desert climate.*

adj. regional *adv.* regionally

sequence
noun

• •

exception
noun

order
*The numbers in the code have to be entered in the right **sequence**.*
v. sequence *adj.* sequential, sequenced *adv.* sequentially

• •

something that is not like others of its type; an anomaly
*Most mammals give birth to live young; the platypus, which
lays eggs, is an **exception**.*
adj. exceptional *adv.* exceptionally

topic
noun

• •

principle
noun

a subject for study or discussion
*The **topic** of her paper is animal life in rainforests.*
adj. topical *adv.* topically

. . . .

an idea that forms the foundation of a theory or of a system of morality
*The **principle** of equality is an important part of true democracy.*
adj. principled

boon
noun

. . . .

fracas
noun

blessing, something to be thankful for
*Dirk realized that his new coworker's computer skills would be a real **boon** to the company.*

• •

noisy dispute
*When the players discovered that the other team was cheating, a violent **fracas** ensued.*

policy
noun

consequently
adverb

a procedure for dealing with or approach to a public issue
*The administration is developing a new **policy** on immigration.*

. . . .

as a result, for this reason, therefore, accordingly
*Regular exercise leads to better health and **consequently** to a longer life.*
n. consequence *adj.* consequent

subsequently
adverb

. . . .

definitely
adverb

following this, later, afterwards, thereafter
*She retired from her banking job at age 65 and **subsequently**
became involved in charity work.*
adj. subsequent

• •

certainly, assuredly
*It is **definitely** going to be sunny tomorrow.*
adj. definite, definitive *adv.* definitively

nevertheless
adverb

. . . .

initially
adverb

in spite of that, nonetheless

*Educational opportunities for women were limited in the nine-teenth century; **nevertheless**, women contributed to that era's scientific accomplishments.*

. . . .

in the beginning, to begin with, at the start

*The cost of owning a car turned out to be much higher than we **initially** expected.*

adj. initial

furthermore
adverb

. . . .

overall
adverb

in addition, additionally, moreover
*She likes the biology program at that university, and **furthermore**, they offered her a scholarship.*

· ·

on the whole, in general
*Sally's Pizza has great crust, but I think Pepe's pizza is better **overall**.*

likewise
adverb

• •

approximately
adverb

similarly; in the same way; also
*I couldn't afford to fly home, and a train ticket was **likewise** beyond my means.*

• •

close to but not precisely, nearly, about
***Approximately** 5 percent of Americans commute to work using public transportation.*
v. approximate *n.* approximation *adj.* approximate, approximated

hence
adverb

• •

via
adverb

as a result, therefore, consequently
*Filtering the water in the aquarium will make it cleaner and **hence** healthier for your fish.*

● ●

by way of
*We flew back from Los Angeles **via** Chicago.*

eventually
adverb

. . . .

recently
adverb

in the end, ultimately
*He can only say a few words now, but **eventually** he will be able to speak fluently.*
n. eventuality *adj.* eventual

. . . .

in the not too distant past, not long ago
*I have always been very healthy, but I **recently** started feeling sick.*
adj. recent

chiefly
adverb

· ·

thereby
adverb

mostly, mainly, primarily
*The book focuses **chiefly** on social history.*

• •

in this way; as a result of this
*He came in second in the race and **thereby** earned a spot on the national team.*